Times to Remember™

*The Fun and Easy Way to Memorize
the Multiplication Tables*

Sandra J. Warren

Illustrations by Juan José Vásquez

Times to Remember

The Fun and Easy Way to Memorize the Multiplication Tables

ISBN: 978-0-9836580-0-9

Author: *Sandra J Warren*
Illustration concepts, ideas & basic design: *Sandra J. Warren*
Illustrations by: *Juan José Vásquez*
Editorial Assistance: *Sharon Millwood, Glenn Boyd*

First Edition: March 2012

ACKNOWLEDGEMENTS

First and always I thank God for His continued guidance and direction. A special thank you to the 3rd and 4th grade students and teachers of The Santiago Christian School, especially to Mindy Seeman and her class who showed such enthusiasm for the project. Thank you for coming up with a better rhyme for 4x8 and giving me permission to use it in this book. A warm thank you to Jake, a 2nd grader, who suggested adding more hidden numbers in the illustrations "because they're really fun to find," and Cynthia, a 5th grader, who reviewed the illustrations offering incredibly professional advise. I also thank Paula, a 2008 SCS graduate, for her faith in the project as well as creating one of the first sketches for 6x8. I feel grateful for the support of my family and friends, including my writing "group," Glenn and Jacqui.

I am indebted to Juan José Vasquez for making this book possible; for sharing his time, talent, patience, kindness, and friendship. Thank you Juan José. Your spiritual gifts are as obvious as your artistic gifts.

I dedicate this book to
my favorite third-grade teacher, my mother
~ **Barbara A. Pierro** ~

A MATTER OF FACT

Learning multiplication may seem like a chore.

Perhaps you even think it's a bore.

Does it make your mind boggle;

even wiggle and woggle?

There is nothing to fear!

It's easier than appears.

If you know 3x2 equals six,

then you'll know 2x3 lickety-split.

The answer is six because the factors remain.

Switching the order keeps the answers the same!

Multiplication facts all work this way.

What a relief. Hip hip horray!

Now you know it's simple to do.

When you learn one fact, you've really learned 2!

TABLE OF CONTENTS

What is Multiplication? **6**

Section 1 Getting started **7**

    Review of the 0, 1, 2 and 5 Tables 8

Section 2 Illustrated Rhymes **13**

    The 3 Times Table 16

    The 4 Times Table 31

    The 6 Times Table 47

    The 7 Times Table 59

    The 8 Times Table 69

    The 9 Times Table 77

Common finger trick for the 9 Times Table **83**

Feedback **84**

WHAT IS MULTIPLICATION?

Multiplication is simply repeated addition. It is a fast way to add numbers in a set. For example, you can add 4+4+4+4+4+4+4 and find the sum of 28. But adding all of those numbers takes time. When you memorize the multiplication tables, you will know 4x7=28. So instead of adding the number 4 again and again 7 times, you will know the answer instantly!

Once you memorize the basic multiplication facts using the fun pictures and rhymes in this book, you will be amazed at how you can add multiples of numbers so quickly!

DID YOU KNOW?

Factor— numbers that are multiplied
3 x 4 = 12; 3 and 4 are factors

Equation—a number sentence
Ex. 7 x 8 = 56

Zero Property of Multiplication—the product of any number and zero is zero.
Ex. 9 x 0 = 0

Product—the answer to a multiplication problem
3 x 4 = 12; 12 is the product

Associative (Grouping) Property of Multiplication—When the grouping of factors in a multiplication problem is changed, the product will remain the same.
Ex. (4 x 2) x 5 = 8 x 5 = 40; 4 x (2 x 5) = 4 x 10 = 40

Commutative (Order) Property of Multiplication—Numbers can be multiplied in any order and the product will be the same.
3 x 8 = 24; 8 x 3 = 24

Identity Property of Multiplication or Property of One— The product of any number and 1 is that number.
Ex. 8 x 1 = 8

Fact Family for Multiplication—a set of related multiplication and division sentences using the same numbers.
3 x 4 = 12   12 ÷ 3 = 4
4 x 3 = 12   12 ÷ 4 = 3

Section 1

Getting Started

0, 1, 2, and 5 Tables

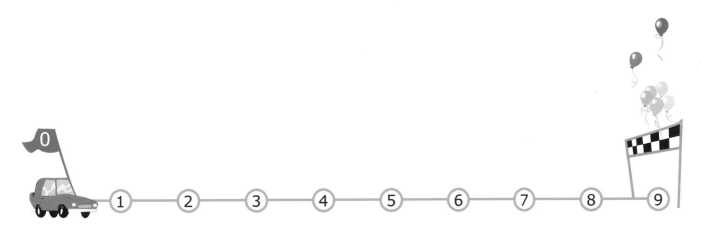

GETTING STARTED: 0, 1, 2, AND 5 TABLES

Before you begin the illustrated rhymes review the tables below, and when you know them, turn the page... get ready, set... and go!

The Zero Times Table

0X0=0	0X5=0
0X1=0	0X6=0
0X2=0	0X7=0
0X3=0	0X8=0
0X4=0	0X9=0

Hint: In multiplication, Zero is always the hero!... Zero wins every time!

The One Times Table

1X0=0	1X5=5
1X1=1	1X6=6
1X2=2	1X7=7
1X3=3	1X8=8
1X4=4	1X9=9

Hint: In multiplication, One is always the loser. The other number always wins!

The Two Times Table

2X0=0	2X5=10
2X1=2	2X6=12
2X2=4	2X7=14
2X3=6	2X8=16
2X4=8	2X9=18

2X1= + 1
         1
        ───
         2

2X2= + 2
         2
        ───
         4

2X3= + 3
         3
        ───
         6

Hint: Two is as easy as a double scoop of ice cream. You just add the other number to itself! Mmmmm, I like it!

The Five Times Table

Let's practice skip counting!

5 10 15 20 25 30 35 40 45 50
55 60 65 70 75 80 85 90 95 100

The Five Times Table (continued)

Hint: *Give me* **FIVE,** *clap it loud, give me* **FIVE,** *count it out. How many times? Let's rap.*

5X1=5	
5X2=10	
5X3=15	
5X4=20	

Now let's clap and rap:

5X5=25	For 5x5, clapping by 5's takes too long, so let just rap it like a song. Cool... 5x5=25 already rhymes!

♫ 5 TIMES 5 EQUALS 25

5 TIMES 5 EQUALS 25 ♫

The Five Times Table

What should we do about 5x6?

...For this and others we have cool tricks.

Hint: *See the pattern? Whenever you have an even number multiplied by 5, just divide the* **even number** *in half and add a* **0.**

$$5X2=10 \qquad 5X4=20 \qquad 5X6=30 \qquad 5X8=40$$

Let's practice 5x6. Half of 6 is 3. Add a zero to get 30. So now we know **5X6=30.** Can you practice 5x8 on your own? What is half of 8? Now add a zero. Yes, you can do it!

What about 5x7 or 5x9?

It's easy. With odd numbers the answer will always end in 5.

Let's practice 5x9. We already know that **5X8=40** (because half of 8 equals 4 and then we add a zero for 40). We know that 5x9 is just one 'clap' higher than 5x8. So just add **5**. Now we know that **5X9=45**

$$5X7=35$$

$$5X9=45$$

DO YOU KNOW?

Question: Why does zero always "win" in multiplication?

Hint: How many groups of apples do you see below?

That's right! There are zero groups of apples. This means you have zero apples in all. You can describe this picture using the equations 0x3=0.

Answer: Zero always "wins" in multiplication because zero groups of anything is always zero! "Zero the Hero" helps you remember the facts in a fun way, but you can also remember that zero groups of anything is always zero!

Question: Why is number one always the 'loser' in multiplication?

Hint: How many groups of 6 apples do we have in the picture below?

That's right! There is one group of 6 apples, or 1x6.
One group of 6 apples means that you have 6 apples in all, or 1x6=6.
You can also think of it as six groups of one (1+1+1+1+1+1).

Answer: When you multiply a number by one it means one group of that number.

Can you think of two multiplication equations for each picture below?

Check your answers on the bottom of the page.

A.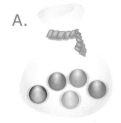

B.

C.

12

Section 2
Illustrated Rhymes

3, 4, 6, 7, 8, and 9 times tables

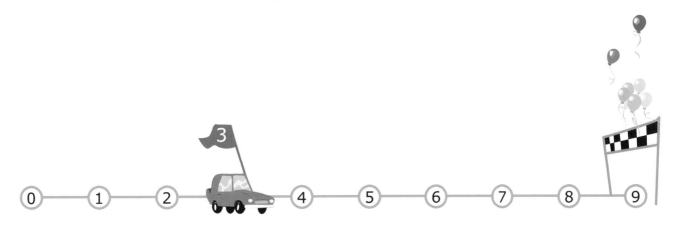

SECTION 2 INSTRUCTIONS

Prepare!

- Since all illustrated rhymes begin with the smaller factor, there is only one for each number set. For example, you will find an illustrated rhyme for 6x8=48, but not for 8x6=48.

- When solving an equation that begins with the larger factor, just think or say the smaller factor first to remember the rhyme and the answer.

- Good news! Did you know that you can learn 4 equations from only one illustrated rhyme? Two for multiplication, and later, two for division!

Begin!

Step 1: **Look** carefully at a picture and rhyme. Describe, or think about what you see. Find the hidden numbers.

Step 2: **Say, then sing or rap** the rhyme several times.

Step 3: **Review** by closing your book (or closing your eyes) and repeating the number fact or rhyme without looking.

If you have the book ***Times to Remember, the Fun and Easy Way to Memorize the Multiplication Tables: Home and Classroom Resources***, then color the black and white picture rhyme that you just studied. Follow the directions in the resource book.

Use the flash cards and quizzes in the resource book to help you remember all of the multiplication facts.

If you have ***Times to Remember, The Fun and Easy Way to Memorize the Multiplication Tables: Sing-Along Songs***, play it and sing along as often as you can.

The 3 Times Table

LET'S REVIEW WHAT WE'VE LEARNED SO FAR

Equation	Hint	Answer page
3X0=__		8
3X1=__		8
3X2=__		9

SEE IT! SAY IT! SING IT!

🎵 Three times three,
Valentine, be mine!
Three times three equals nine. 🎵

3x3
Valentine, be mine!

$$3 \times 3 = 9$$

SEE IT! SAY IT! SING IT!

♪ **Three times four, busy little elves, three times four equals twelve.** ♪

3x4
busy little elves,
3×4=12

SEE IT! SAY IT! SING IT!

♫ Give me five, clap it loud,
give me five, count it out!
Three times, let's rap! 5, 10, 15! ♫
Three times five equals fifteen.

Note: The five times table is in section 1 of the Sing-Along Songs.

3×5=15

SEE IT! SAY IT! SING IT!

♪ **Three times six, making great ice cream, three times six equals eighteen.** ♪

3x6

making great ice cream,

3×6=18

three x seven=21   3

3x_=21

_x7=21   x7
            ?

SEE IT! SAY IT! SING IT!

♪ Three times seven, ♪ sailing in the sun, three times seven equals twenty-one.

?
x7
21   3x7=21   ?x7=21

3
three x seven=21   x 7
            21

3x7

sailing in the sun,

$3 \times 7 = 21$

three x eight=24

3×_=24   3

_×8=24   ×8
         ?

SEE IT! SAY IT! SING IT!

♪ Three times eight, hopping to the store, three times eight equals twenty-four. ♪

?
×8
24
    3×8=24   ?×8=24

            3
            ×8
three x eight=24
            24

3x8
hopping to the store,
$3 \times 8 = 24$

SEE IT! SAY IT! SING IT!

♪ **Three times nine, flying to heaven, three times nine equals twenty-seven.** ♪

3x9

flying to heaven,

$3 \times 9 = 27$

FUN REVIEW

A   3
      × 1

B   3
      × 9

C   3
      × 2

D   3
      × 4

E   3
      × 3

F   3
      × 8

G   3
      × ⬤

H   3
      × 7

I   3
      × 5

J   3
      × 6

A) 3 B) 27 C) 6 D) 12 E) 9 F) 24 G) 0 H) 21 I) 15 J) 18

The 4 Times Table

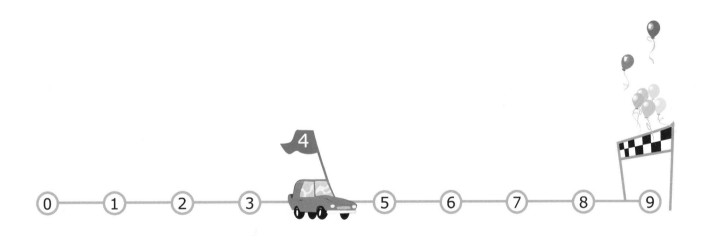

MULTIPLICATION RIDDLE

Solve the puzzle and discover the message!

2 x 5	2 x 4	5 x10

3 x 5	3 x 7	3 x 2

USE A PIECE OF SCRAP PAPER TO HELP YOU. WRITE THE ANSWERS TO THE EQUATIONS, THEN WRITE THE CORRESPONDING LETTERS FROM THE "KEY."

4 x 8	4 x 7	0 x 3	3 x 4	5 x 6

KEY

0	6	8	10	12	15	21	28	30	32	50
E	D	O	Y	A	D	I	R	T	G	U

LET'S REVIEW WHAT WE'VE LEARNED SO FAR

Be sure to SING or RAP the rhymes from memory. (Look for the ♪.)

Equation	Hint	Answer page
$4 \times 0 = \underline{}$		8
$4 \times 1 = \underline{}$		8
$4 \times 2 = \underline{}$		9
$4 \times 3 = \underline{}$		19

SEE IT! SAY IT! SING IT!

♪ Four times four, ♪ little brothers start to scream, four times four equals sixteen.

SEE IT! SAY IT! SING IT!

♪ Four times four, ♪ little brothers start to scream, four times four equals sixteen.

34

4x4
little brothers
start to scream,

4×4=16

SEE IT! SAY IT! SING IT!

♪ Give me five, clap it loud,
give me five, count it out!
Four times, let's rap! 5, 10, 15, 20!
Four times five equals twenty. ♪

Note: The five times table is in section 1 of the Sing-Along Songs.

$$4 \times 5 = 20$$

SEE IT! SAY IT! SING IT!

♪ **Four times six,**
sleeping on the shore,
four times six equals twenty-four. ♪

4x6

sleeping on the shore,

$$4 \times 6 = 24$$

SEE IT! SAY IT! SING IT!

♪ **Four times seven, jumping over two gates, four times seven equals twenty-eight.** ♪

40

4x7

jumping over two gates,

$$4 \times 7 = 28$$

SEE IT! SAY IT! SING IT!

♪ Four times eight, ♪
singing tootie whoooooooooo!!!
Four times eight equals thirty-two.

4x8
singing tootie
whoooooooooo!!!
4×8=32

SEE IT! SAY IT! SING IT!

♪ **Four times nine, wrap the birthday gifts, four times nine equals thirty-six.** ♪

44

4x9

wrap the birthday gifts,

4 × 9 = 36

FUN REVIEW

$$\begin{array}{r} 4 \\ \times\,2 \\ \hline \end{array}$$ A

$$\begin{array}{r} 4 \\ \times\,9 \\ \hline \end{array}$$ B

$$\begin{array}{r} 4 \\ \times\,5 \\ \hline \end{array}$$ C

$$\begin{array}{r} 4 \\ \times\,8 \\ \hline \end{array}$$ D

$$\begin{array}{r} 4 \\ \times\,0 \\ \hline \end{array}$$ E

$$\begin{array}{r} 4 \\ \times\,7 \\ \hline \end{array}$$ F

$$\begin{array}{r} 4 \\ \times\,6 \\ \hline \end{array}$$ G

$$\begin{array}{r} 4 \\ \times\,1 \\ \hline \end{array}$$ H

$$\begin{array}{r} 4 \\ \times\,4 \\ \hline \end{array}$$ I

$$\begin{array}{r} 4 \\ \times\,3 \\ \hline \end{array}$$ J

46

The 6 Times Table

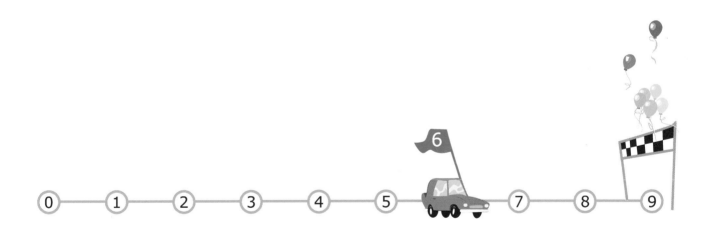

A-MAZING TIMES!

Solve the multiplication problems to complete the maze. Look for answers that are even numbers in order to find the correct way!

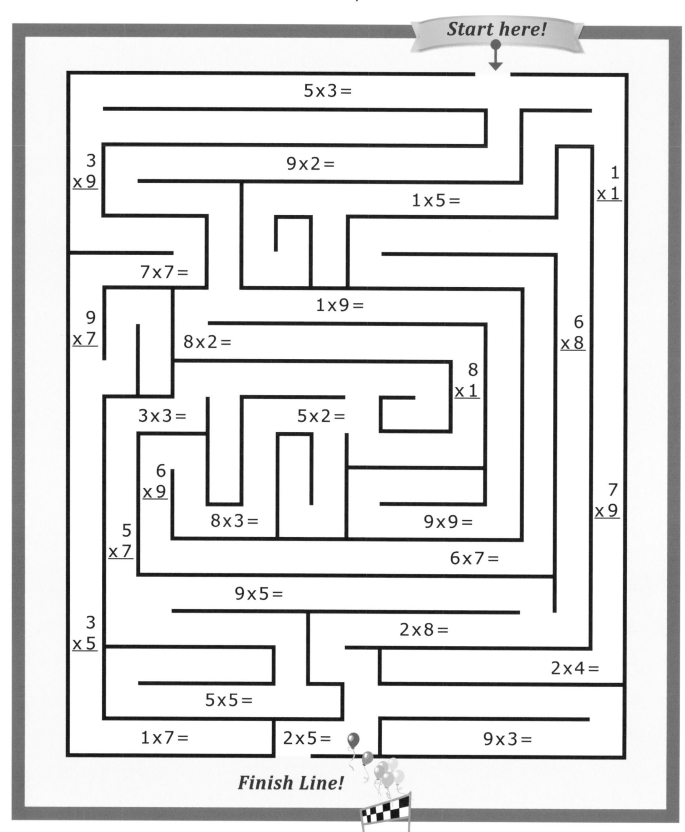

Start here!

5x3=

3 x9

9x2=

1x5=

1 x1

7x7=

1x9=

9 x7

8x2=

6 x8

8 x1

3x3=

5x2=

6 x9

5 x7

8x3=

9x9=

7 x9

6x7=

9x5=

3 x5

2x8=

2x4=

5x5=

1x7=

2x5=

9x3=

Finish Line!

LET'S REVIEW WHAT WE'VE LEARNED SO FAR

Be sure to SING or RAP the rhymes from memory. (Look for the ♪.)

Equation	Hint	Answer page
6X0=__		8
6X1=__		8
6X2=__		9
6X3=__		23
6X4=__		39
6X5=__		11

SEE IT! SAY IT! SING IT!

♪ ♪

Six times six,
so thirsty and sick,
six times six equals thirty-six.

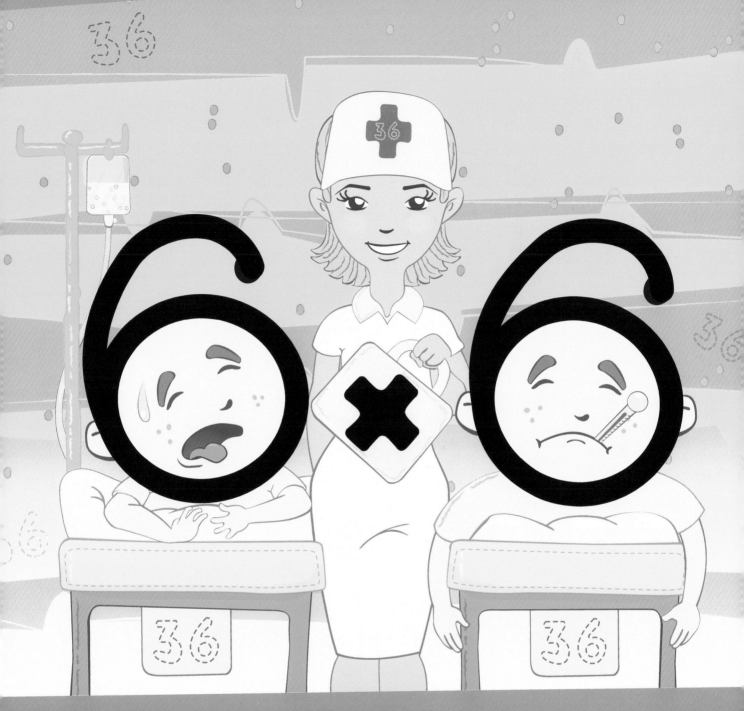

6x6

so **thirsty** and **sick,**

6×6=36

6x_=42

six x seven=42

6
x 7
?

_x7=42

SEE IT! SAY IT! SING IT!

♪ **Six times seven, having tea for two, six times seven equals forty-two.** ♪

?
x 7
42

6x7=42

?x7=42

six x seven=42

6
x 7
42

6x7

having tea for two,

6×7=42

SEE IT! SAY IT! SING IT!

🎵 Six times eight, went out for a date, six times eight equals forty-eight. 🎵

54

6x8
went out for a date,

6×8=48

six x nine=54

6x__=54

6
x 9
—
?

__x9=54

SEE IT! SAY IT! SING IT!

♪ **Six times nine, catching fish galore, six times nine equals fifty-four.** ♪

?
x 9
—
54

6x9=54

?x9=54

six x nine=54

6
x 9
—
54

6x9

catching fish galore,

6×9=54

FUN REVIEW

$$\begin{array}{r} 6 \\ \times\ 3 \\ \hline \end{array}$$ **A**

$$\begin{array}{r} 6 \\ \times\ 1 \\ \hline \end{array}$$ **B**

$$\begin{array}{r} 6 \\ \times\ 4 \\ \hline \end{array}$$ **C**

$$\begin{array}{r} 6 \\ \times\ 8 \\ \hline \end{array}$$ **D**

$$\begin{array}{r} 6 \\ \times\ 0 \\ \hline \end{array}$$ **E**

$$\begin{array}{r} 6 \\ \times\ 9 \\ \hline \end{array}$$ **F**

$$\begin{array}{r} 6 \\ \times\ 7 \\ \hline \end{array}$$ **G**

$$\begin{array}{r} 6 \\ \times\ 2 \\ \hline \end{array}$$ **H**

$$\begin{array}{r} 6 \\ \times\ 5 \\ \hline \end{array}$$ **I**

$$\begin{array}{r} 6 \\ \times\ 6 \\ \hline \end{array}$$ **J**

The 7 Times Table

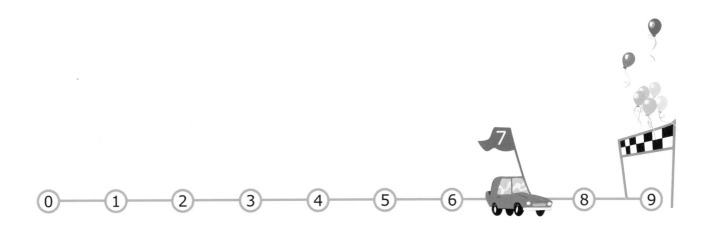

LET'S REVIEW WHAT WE'VE LEARNED SO FAR

Be sure to SING or RAP the rhymes from memory. (Look for the ♪.)

Equation	Hint	Answer Page
7 X 0 = __		8
7 X 1 = __		8
7 X 2 = __		9
7 X 3 = __		25

Equation	Hint	Answer Page
7X4=__		41
7X5=__		11
7X6=__		53

seven x seven=49

7x_=49

7
x 7
?

_x7=49

SEE IT! SAY IT! SING IT!

♪ Seven times seven, ♪ looking so fine, seven times seven equals forty-nine.

?
x 7
49

7x7=49

?x7=49

7
x 7
49

seven x seven=49

62

7×7
looking so fine,
7×7=49

seven x eight=56

7x_=56

7
x 8
?

_x8=56

SEE IT! SAY IT! SING IT!

🎵 Seven times eight, 🎵
in a sugar cookie mix,
seven times eight equals fifty-six.

?
x 8
56

7x8=56

?x8=56

7
x 8
56

seven x eight=56

7x8
in a sugar cookie mix,
7×8=56

SEE IT! SAY IT! SING IT!

♪ Seven times nine, candy sticks for me! ♪
seven times nine equals sixty-three.

7x9
candy sticks for me!

7×9=63

FUN REVIEW

$$\begin{array}{r} 7 \\ \times\ 3 \\ \hline \end{array}\quad\textbf{A}$$

$$\begin{array}{r} 7 \\ \times\ 9 \\ \hline \end{array}\quad\textbf{B}$$

$$\begin{array}{r} 7 \\ \times\ 5 \\ \hline \end{array}\quad\textbf{C}$$

$$\begin{array}{r} 7 \\ \times\ 8 \\ \hline \end{array}\quad\textbf{D}$$

$$\begin{array}{r} 7 \\ \times\ 7 \\ \hline \end{array}\quad\textbf{E}$$

$$\begin{array}{r} 7 \\ \times\ 4 \\ \hline \end{array}\quad\textbf{F}$$

$$\begin{array}{r} 7 \\ \times\ 1 \\ \hline \end{array}\quad\textbf{J}$$

$$\begin{array}{r} 7 \\ \times\ 0 \\ \hline \end{array}\quad\textbf{G}$$

$$\begin{array}{r} 7 \\ \times\ 2 \\ \hline \end{array}\quad\textbf{H}$$

$$\begin{array}{r} 7 \\ \times\ 6 \\ \hline \end{array}\quad\textbf{I}$$

A) 21 B) 63 C) 35 D) 56 E) 49 F) 28 G) 0 H) 14 I) 42 J) 7

The 8 Times Table

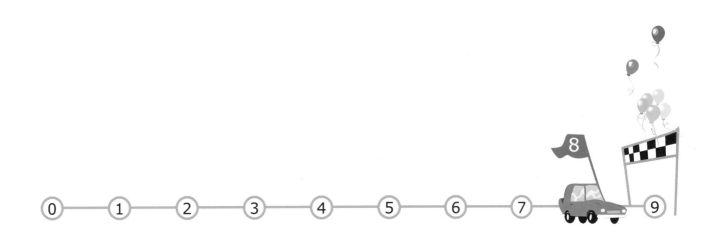

LET'S REVIEW WHAT WE'VE LEARNED SO FAR

Be sure to SING or RAP the rhymes from memory. (Look for the ♫.)

Equation	Hint	Answer page
8X0=___		8
8X1=___		8
8X2=___		9
8X3=___		27

Equation	Hint	Answer page
8X4=___		43
8X5=___		11
8X6=___		55
8X7=___		65

SEE IT! SAY IT! SING IT!

♪ **Eight times eight, go out the sticky door, eight times eight equals sixty-four.** ♪

8x8
go out the sticky door,
8×8=64

eight x nine=72

8x_=72

_x9=72

8
x 9

?

SEE IT! SAY IT! SING IT!

♪ Eight times nine, we're almost through! ♪
Eight times nine equals seventy-two.

?
x 9

72

8x9=72

?x9=72

8
x 9

72

eight x nine=72

8x9
we're almost through!
8×9=72

FUN REVIEW

8
x 7
A

8
x 0
B

8
x 2
C

8
x 8
D

8
x 5
E

8
x 3
F

8
x 6
G

8
x 1
H

8
x 4
I

8
x 9
J

The 9 Times Table

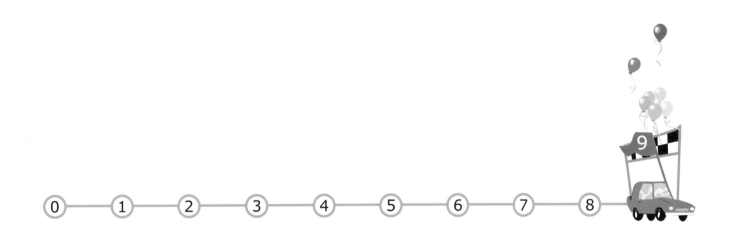

LET'S REVIEW WHAT WE'VE LEARNED SO FAR

Be sure to SING or RAP the rhymes from memory. (Look for the ♩.)

Equation	Hint	Answer page
9X0=__		8
9X1=__		8
9X2=__		9
9X3=__		29
9X4=__		45

Equation	Hint	Answer page
9X5=__		11
9X6=__		57
9X7=__		67
9X8=__		75

nine x nine=81

9x_=81

9
x 9
—
?

_X9=81

SEE IT! SAY IT! SING IT!

♪ Nine times nine,
hooray, we're done!
Nine times nine equals eighty-one. ♪

?
x 9
—
81

9x9=81

?x9=81

nine x nine=81

9
x 9
—
81

80

9x9
hooray, we're done!

9×9=81

COMMON FINGER TRICK FOR THE 9 TIMES TABLE

Boys and Girls,

Perhaps you already know this trick. Simply place all your fingers on the piano keys, or just use the keys to count if you wish.

Whenever you have a number multiplied by nine, you can use this trick. Let's practice 9x6. Lift your number 6 finger (your thumb). How many fingers are still on the keys to the left of that finger? Looks like 5. How many to the right? Looks like 4.

Now bring them together and you get 54.

Now you can practice on your own!

9X1=9	9X2=18	9X3=27
9X4=36	9X5=45	9X6=54
9X7=63	9X8=72	9X9=81

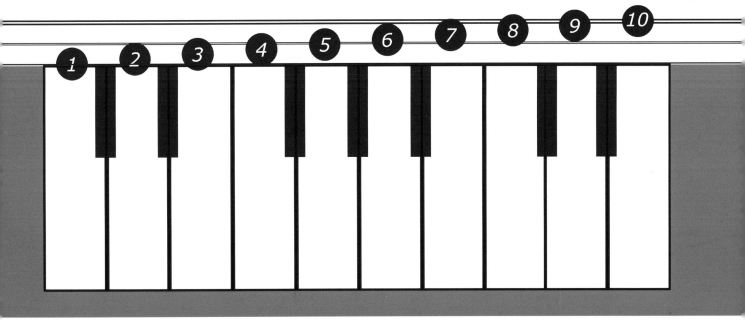

Although the 9-table finger trick can help you when you get stuck, many students find the *Times to Remember* picture rhymes work even better. As well, the picture rhymes teach fact families. Fact families are number sets that belong together. In multiplication and division, for example, 6,9 and 54 belong together. When you remember a fact family such as this, you can solve four math equations!

Two Multiplication Equations!   and later...   *Two Division Equations!*

6x9=54   9x6=54   54÷6=9   54÷9=6   **83**

FEEDBACK

Dear Students,

Congratulations! You have just completed this entire book of multiplication rhymes, pictures, and more. I hope when you are asked the times tables your mind won't boggle, wiggle, or woggle! Hopefully you are quicker and more confident solving those pesky facts. How much did it help you? What did you like best about *Times to Remember?* I would like to know your thoughts, opinions, and ideas. Your input is important as it could help make *Times to Remember* products even better.

You can send your letter to this address:

Ms. Sandra Warren
Joyful Learning Publications, LLC
Suite 153 3148 Plainfield Ave, N.E.
Grand Rapids, Michigan 49525-3285

If you have enjoyed *Times to Remember* and found it helpful, please let others know about it so they can benefit as well.

Have a Joyful Day!

Teacher Sandy

Teacher Sandy
www.TheTimesTable.com

ABOUT THE AUTHOR

SANDRA WARREN, mother of three, enjoys finding ways to help students learn using songs, skits, games and more. She taught for several years in the Dominican Republic, teaching elementary math at a bilingual school and middle school science at an American-accredited Christian school. A certified secondary biology teacher, she received her Masters of Science Degree in Education in 2011. After 11 years living overseas, Sandra and her family have relocated to Michigan where she plans to research, write, and share ideas to help parents, teachers, and children.